Differentiated Reading
for Comprehension
Grade 6

Credits

Content Editor: Nancy Rogers Bosse
Copy Editor: Karen Seberg
Illustrations: Nick Greenwood, Donald O'Connor

Visit *carsondellosa.com* for correlations to Common Core, state, national, and Canadian provincial standards.

Carson-Dellosa Publishing, LLC
PO Box 35665
Greensboro, NC 27425 USA
carsondellosa.com

Printed in the USA • All rights reserved.   ISBN 978-1-4838-0490-3

01-034141151

Table of Contents

Introduction

Providing all students access to high quality, nonfiction text is essential to Common Core State Standards mastery. This book contains exactly what teachers are looking for: high-interest nonfiction passages, each written at three different reading levels, followed by a shared set of text-dependent comprehension questions and a writing prompt to build content knowledge. Both general academic and domain-specific vocabulary words are reinforced at the end of each passage for further comprehension support. The standards listed on each page provide an easy reference tool for lesson planning, and the Common Core Alignment Chart on page 3 allows you to target or remediate specific skills.

The book is comprised of 15 stories that are written at three levels:
- Below level (one dot beside the page number): 1 to 1.5 levels below grade level
- On level (two dots beside the page number): 0 to 0.5 levels below grade level
- Advanced (three dots beside the page number): 1 to 2 levels above grade level

Which students will not enjoy reading about the unusual puffin or spy planes or the ancient city of Pompeii? This book will quickly become the go-to resource for differentiated nonfiction reading practice in your classroom!

Common Core Alignment Chart

Common Core State Standards*		Practice Pages
Reading Standards for Informational Text		
Key Ideas and Details	6.RI.1–6.RI.3	7, 15, 23, 31, 39, 43, 47, 51, 55, 59
Craft and Structure	6.RI.4–6.RI.6	4–6, 8–10, 12–14, 15, 16–18, 20–22, 24–26, 27, 28–30, 32–34, 35, 36–38, 39, 40–42, 43, 44–46, 48–50, 52–54, 56–58, 60–62, 63
Integration of Knowledge and Ideas	6.RI.7–6.RI.9	11, 47, 63
Range of Reading and Level of Text Complexity	6.RI.10	4–6, 8–10, 12–14, 16–18, 20–22, 24–26, 28–30, 32–34, 36–38, 40–42, 44–46, 48–50, 52–54, 56–58, 60–62
Writing Standards		
Text Types and Purposes	6.W.1–6.W.3	7, 15, 19, 23, 27, 31, 35, 39, 43, 47, 51, 55, 59, 63
Production and Distribution of Writing	6.W.4–6.W.6	7, 31, 43
Research to Build and Present Knowledge	6.W.7–6.W.9	11, 27, 47, 59, 63
Range of Writing	6.W.10	11, 23
Language Standards		
Conventions of Standard English	6.L.1–6.L.2	19, 23, 51
Knowledge of Language	6.L.3	11, 47, 55
Vocabulary Acquisition and Use	6.L.4–6.L.6	4–6, 7, 8–10, 12–14, 15, 16–18, 19, 20–22, 24–26, 27, 28–30, 31, 32–34, 35, 36–38, 39, 40–42, 43, 44–46, 48–50, 51, 52–54, 55, 56–58, 59, 60–62, 63

* © Copyright 2010. National Governors Association Center for Best Practices and Council of Chief State School Officers. All rights reserved.

How to Use This Alignment Chart

The Common Core State Standards for English Language Arts are a shared set of expectations for each grade level in the areas of reading, writing, speaking, listening, and language. They define what students should understand and be able to do. This chart presents the standards that are covered in this book.

Use this chart to plan your instruction, practice, or remediation of a specific standard. To do this, first choose your targeted standard; then, find the pages listed on the chart that correlate to the standard you are teaching. Finally, assign the reading pages and follow-up questions to practice the skill.

Is It a Bird? Is It a Fish?

Explorers crossing the Atlantic Ocean saw an **extraordinary** creature. It was a fish with wings like a bird! Or, wait; was it a bird that swam like a fish? This strange creature with a clown-like beak could be seen using its black wings to dive deep into the ocean waters or to fly rapidly through the sky. To confuse matters even more, this unusual "fish bird" made a strange, growling sound like a mooing cow. The explorers feared this small beast. They invented stories that this animal had been born from pieces of wood that came from shipwrecks.

Today, this seabird is no longer feared, in part because scientists have studied the creature to learn more about it. They have learned that this animal, now known as the Atlantic **puffin**, is a seabird that likes the ice-cold ocean water near Iceland. These amazing ocean-loving birds seem to fly underwater. They use their wings to dive deep into the sea where they catch small fish to eat. A puffin usually catches about 10 fish during one dive. One scientist saw a puffin catch 62 little fish during a dive! A puffin spends most of its life on the water. When it is not diving for food, it floats on the cold waves of the sea. Young puffins spend years at sea without ever coming to land.

The puffin does not always live in the sea. It lives on land when it is hatching and raising its chicks. The birds like rocky cliffs where they build **burrows** instead of nests. This gives them a place to lay eggs out of the cold wind and rain. On land, the puffin is not as graceful as it is in the water. It waddles out of its burrow and hops from rock to rock. The puffin can also fly. It flies fast—up to 55 miles per hour (88.51 kmh).

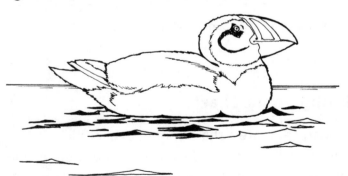

The puffin is about 10 inches tall. Its feathers are black and white. It has a big, brightly colored beak. Its orange webbed feet look like duck feet. It has yellow eyes. Puffins are often called "sea parrots."

extraordinary: beyond what is normal or expected
puffin: a seabird
burrow: shelter made by an animal

Is It a Bird? Is It a Fish?

Explorers discovering new lands across the Atlantic Ocean saw an **extraordinary** creature. It was a fish with wings like a bird! Or, wait; was it a bird that swam like a fish? This strange creature with a clown-like beak could be seen using its black wings to dive deep into the ocean waters or to fly rapidly through the sky. To confuse matters even more, this unusual "fish bird" made a strange, deep sound like a mooing cow. The explorers feared this small beast. They invented stories that this animal had been born from pieces of wood that came from shipwrecks.

Today, these seabirds are no longer feared, in part because scientists have studied to learn more about them. Now known as the Atlantic **puffin**, this seabird enjoys living in the ice-cold ocean water near Iceland. These amazing ocean-loving birds seem to fly underwater using their wings to dive deep into the sea where they feed on small fish. A puffin usually catches about 10 fish during one dive, although one scientist witnessed a puffin catching 62 small fish in one dive! A puffin spends most of its life on the water. When it is not diving for food, it floats on the cold waves of the sea. Young puffins spend years at sea without ever coming to land.

The puffin does not always live in the sea. It lives on land when it is hatching and raising its chicks. The birds build **burrows** instead of nests in the high rocky crags of the cliffs along the ocean shores. These provide a place to protect their eggs from the cold wind and rain. In the water, the puffin is quite graceful, but, on the land, it waddles and hops from rock to rock. The puffin can fly at speeds up to 55 miles per hour (88.51 kmh).

The puffin is about 10 inches tall. Its feathers are black and white. It has a big, brightly colored beak. Its orange webbed feet look like duck feet. It has yellow eyes. Puffins are often called "sea parrots."

extraordinary: beyond what is normal or expected
puffin: a seabird
burrow: shelter made by an animal

Is It a Bird? Is It a Fish?

Explorers discovering new lands across the Atlantic Ocean saw an **extraordinary** creature—a fish that **propelled** itself through the ocean waters with wings like a bird! Or, wait; was it a bird that lived in the ocean waters like a fish? This strange clown-like creature with its bright orange beak and black feathers was seen using its wings at one moment to dive deep into the ocean waters and then to fly rapidly through the sky. To confuse the explorers even more, this unusual "fish bird" made strange, deep **guttural** sounds like a mooing cow. Because the explorers feared this mythical creature, they invented tales that portrayed it as rising from pieces of wood from shipwrecks.

Today these seabirds are no longer feared, in part because scientists have studied to learn more about them. Now known as the Atlantic puffin, this seabird enjoys a habitat in the ice-cold ocean water near Iceland. These ocean-loving birds seem to fly underwater using their wings to dive deep into the sea where they feed on small fish. A puffin usually catches about 10 fish during one dive, although one scientist witnessed a puffin catching 62 small fish in one dive! Puffins spend the majority of their lives on the water. When they are not diving for food, they float contentedly on the cold ocean waves. Young puffins spend years at sea without ever coming to land.

When it is time to hatch and raise their chicks, the birds build **burrows** in the high rocky crags of the cliffs along the ocean edge. These provide a place to protect their eggs from the cold wind and rain. In the water, puffins are quite graceful, but, on the land, they waddle and hop from rock to rock. In the air, puffins can fly at speeds up to 55 miles per hour (88.51 kmh).

The puffin is about 10 inches tall. Its feathers are black and white. It has a big, brightly colored beak. Its orange webbed feet look like duck feet. It has yellow eyes. Puffins are often called "sea parrots."

extraordinary: beyond what is normal or expected
propelled: moved through water
guttural: a harsh sound made in the throat
burrow: shelter made by an animal

Is It a Bird? Is It a Fish?

Answer the questions.

1. Using words from the passage, write at least two synonyms for *extraordinary*.
   _____

2. Why did the early explorers fear the puffin?
   _____

3. Circle two phrases that best describe a puffin.

   lives mostly at sea   clumsy swimmer   land bird   fierce fighter

   good diver   flightless bird   scary bird

   clown-like fish   funny bird   slow flyer

4. What simile is used to describe the sound a puffin makes?
   _____

5. Why does the author say that puffins seem to "fly" underwater?
   _____

6. When does a puffin live on land? Write your answer in a complete sentence.
   _____

7. Write **F** for fact and **O** for opinion beside each statement.

   _____ Puffins build burrows for their chicks.

   _____ Puffins are strange, mythical creatures.

   _____ Puffins live for years without coming to land.

   _____ Puffins are extraordinary birds.

8. Do you think the name *puffin* fits this bird? If so, explain. If not, what name would you use and why?
   _____
   _____

9. Write three details from the passage that tell what a puffin looks like.
   _____
   _____

10. On another sheet of paper, write a story about a puffin. Use facts from the passage to add descriptive details. Share your writing with an adult and then revise your story. Publish your story on the computer.

Don't Mess with the Honey Badger

Don't be fooled by the sweet name of the honey badger. This furry animal is said to be as **ferocious** as a lion, especially at mealtime. Despite its smallness, very few animals of any size want to get in a fight with this **menacing** animal. It has sharp teeth and long claws. It is said to be one of the most feared animals in the world. Scientists think that the honey badger's black, gray, and white skunk-striped fur is a **warning** to stay away.

How tough is the honey badger? Tough enough to take on a large poisonous snake like a cobra. Even a snakebite will not stop the honey badger. It may fall over and sleep for a few hours, only to get up and start looking for food again.

The honey badger is known for its hunting skills. Its long claws help it dig up small animals or eggs underground in just minutes. It is hard for even a fast animal to run away from this super digger. The honey badger also climbs trees to find fruit. It uses its sharp teeth to rip open melons that grow in the wild.

As its name suggests, the honey badger has a real sweet tooth, especially for honey. But, to find honey, the honey badger may have some help. Many people believe that a bird called a honeyguide will lead a honey badger to a beehive. Much like a skunk, the badger uses its scent gland to stun the bees. Then, it claws into the hive to get to the honey. The honeyguide waits in a nearby tree to eat what the honey badger leaves behind.

ferocious: very fierce
menacing: dangerous
warning: signal

Don't Mess with the Honey Badger

Don't be fooled by the sweet name of the honey badger. This furry animal is said to be as **ferocious** as a lion especially at mealtime. Despite its smallness, very few animals of any size want to get in a fight with this **menacing** animal. Its sharp teeth and long claws make it one of the most feared animals in the world. Scientists think that the honey badger's black, gray, and white skunk-striped fur is a **warning** to stay away.

How tough is the honey badger? Tough enough to take on a large poisonous snake like a cobra. Even a snakebite will not stop the honey badger. It may fall over and sleep for a few hours, only to get up and start looking for food again.

The honey badger is known for its hunting skills. Its long claws help it dig up small animals or eggs underground in just minutes. It is hard for even a fast animal to run away from this super digger. The honey badger also climbs trees to find fruit. It uses its sharp teeth to rip open melons that grow in the dry deserts from Africa to India where it lives.

As its name suggests, the honey badger has a real sweet tooth especially for honey. But, to find honey, the honey badger may have a honey-hunting friend—a bird called the greater honeyguide. Many people believe that this bird swoops over a honey badger and leads it to a beehive. The badger uses its scent gland, like a skunk's, to stun the bees. Then, it claws into the hive to get to the honey. The honeyguide waits patiently in a nearby tree to eat what the honey badger leaves behind.

ferocious: very fierce
menacing: dangerous
warning: signal

Don't Mess with the Honey Badger

Don't be fooled by its sweet name; the honey badger is said to be as **ferocious** as a lion, especially at mealtime. Despite its smallness, very few animals of any size want to get in a fight with this **menacing** creature. Its sharp teeth and long claws make this one of the most feared animals in the world. Even its black, gray, and white skunk-striped fur is a natural warning to stay away.

The fearless honey badger is tough enough to take on a large poisonous snake like a cobra. Even a snakebite will not stop the honey badger because of its **resistance** to snake **venom**. If bitten, the honey badger may fall over and sleep for a few hours, only to get up and start hunting for food again.

The honey badger is known for its amazing hunting skills. Its long claws help it dig up small animals or eggs underground in just minutes. It's nearly impossible for even a fast animal like a rabbit to run away from this powerful digger. The honey badger also climbs trees to find fruit. It uses its sharp teeth to rip open melons that grow in the dry deserts from Africa to India where it lives.

As its name suggests, the honey badger has a sweet tooth, especially for honey. But, to find honey, the honey badger may have a honey-hunting friend—a bird called the greater honeyguide. Many people believe that this bird swoops over a honey badger and leads it to a beehive. Then, the honey badger uses its skunk-like scent gland to stun the bees. Finally, it claws into the hive to get to the honey. The honeyguide waits patiently in a nearby tree to eat what the honey badger leaves behind.

ferocious: very fierce
menacing: dangerous
resistance: the ability to not react
venom: poison

Don't Mess with the Honey Badger

Answer the questions.

1. Write three words from this passage that contrast the sweet name of the honey badger to its actual personality.

   _____ _____ _____

2. Scientists think that the honey badger's stripes serve as a warning. Circle the definition of *warning*.

   A. a sign of safety
   C. a dangerous element

   B. a signal of danger
   D. someone who is protected by another

3. To what does the author compare a honey badger? _____

4. Write three words or phrases that describe how the honey badger looks.

   _____

   _____

   _____

5. Describe how many people believe the honey badger and the honeyguide help each other.

   _____

   _____

6. How does the honey badger use its body to get food?

   _____

   _____

7. Write a question you have about the honey badger that is not answered in the passage.

   _____

8. Use the Internet or books to research the answer to the question you wrote in question 7. Write the answer to the question and the location where you found the answer.

   _____

   _____

9. On another sheet of paper, write a report about the honey badger. Include information from the passage and a source you used in question 8. Be sure to edit your report for correct grammar, spelling, and punctuation.

World of Peril

The early life of the green sea turtle is full of **peril**. Only one in 1,000 baby sea turtles **survive** to adulthood. From its nest in the sand, it chips its way out of its egg. It uses an egg tooth, or small horn, on the end of its beak. Its mother is not there to help it. Instead it is greeted by crabs, coyotes, and dogs waiting to eat it for a snack. To survive, the baby turtle must hide in the sand until night. Then, it crawls to the sea.

The small turtle must swim hard against the waves to reach the ocean waters. In the sea, it struggles to find food. It must also keep itself from being food for fish. The little sea turtle swims in the ocean for more than a year before returning to the beach.

As dangerous as the sea turtle's life is against the natural world, its most perilous enemy is the human. The garbage left by humans in the ocean causes problems for the small green sea turtle. A little turtle might choke on a piece of plastic floating in the sea. It might swallow oil floating on the ocean's surface. Young turtles also get trapped in fishing nets. There are laws against hunting sea turtles. Still, many are hunted, both for their meat and for their shells. All of these dangers can be prevented if humans act **responsibly**.

Sea turtles that do survive to grow into adulthood go through many changes. For example, adult green sea turtles weigh about 500 pounds (226.8 kg). They stop eating jellyfish and other meat and eat only plants. And, they may plan a trip to go back home again. A female sea turtle goes back to the beach where she was born. This is the only place where she will lay eggs. Even if it has been 40 years since she was a baby, she always knows her way back home.

peril: danger
survive: to stay alive
responsibly: acting with a clear sense of right and wrong

World of Peril

The early life of the green sea turtle is full of **peril**. Only one in 1,000 baby sea turtles **survive** to adulthood. From its nest in the sand, it chips its way out of its egg using an egg tooth, or small horn, on the end of its beak. Its mother is not there to help it. Instead it is greeted by crabs, coyotes, and dogs waiting to eat it for a snack. To survive, the baby turtle must hide in the sand until night when it can scramble to the sea **undetected**.

The small turtle must swim hard against the waves to reach the ocean waters. In the sea, it struggles to find food. It must also keep itself from being the food of tiger sharks or other fish. The little sea turtle swims in the ocean for more than a year before returning to the beach.

But, as dangerous as the sea turtle's life is against the natural world, its most perilous enemy is the human. The garbage left by humans in the ocean causes problems for the small green sea turtle. A little turtle might choke on a piece of plastic floating in the sea. It might swallow oil floating on the ocean's surface. Young turtles can also get trapped in fishing nets. There are laws against hunting sea turtles. Still, many are hunted, both for their meat and for their shells. All of these dangers can be prevented if humans act **responsibly**.

Sea turtles that do survive the dangers to reach adulthood go through many changes. Adult green sea turtles can grow to about 500 pounds (226.8 kg). They stop eating jellyfish and other meat and eat only plants. And, they may plan a trip to go back home again. A female sea turtle goes back to the beach where she was born. This is the only place where she will lay eggs. Even if it has been 40 years since she was a baby, she always knows her way back home.

peril: danger
survive: to stay alive
undetected: unseen
responsibly: acting with a clear sense of right and wrong

World of Peril

The early life of the green sea turtle is full of **peril**. Only one in 1,000 baby sea turtles survive to adulthood. From its nest in the sand, it chips its way out of its egg using an egg tooth, a small horn on the end of its beak. Its mother is not there to provide help and support; instead, it is greeted by crabs, coyotes, and dogs waiting to consume it for a snack. To survive, the baby turtle must burrow itself in the sand until night when it can scramble to the sea **undetected**.

The small turtle swims **vigorously** against the incoming waves to get away from the dangers of the beach. Once in the ocean, the young sea turtle encounters new dangers. In the sea, it struggles to find food and to keep itself from being the food of tiger sharks or other fish. The little sea turtle will swim in the ocean for a year or more before it crawls up on land again.

But, as dangerous as the sea turtle's life is against the natural world, its most **treacherous** enemy is the human. The garbage left by humans in the ocean causes problems for the small green sea turtle. The little turtle might choke on a piece of plastic floating in the sea or swallow oil floating on the ocean's surface. A young turtle can also get trapped in a fishing net and be unable to free itself. Even though there are laws against hunting sea turtles, many are captured, both for their meat and for their shells. All of these man-made dangers can be prevented if humans act responsibly.

Sea turtles that do survive the dangers to reach adulthood go through many changes. An adult green sea turtle can grow to about 500 pounds (226.8 kg).

peril: danger
undetected: unseen
vigorously: with extreme effort
treacherous: not to be trusted

World of Peril

Answer the questions.

1. Using clues from the passage, what does the word *peril* mean?

   A. beauty   **B.** enjoyment   **C.** danger   **D.** carelessness

2. Write **T** for true or **F** for false.

   _____ A green sea turtle baby stays with its mother for one year.

   _____ The green sea turtle can die if it eats oil.

   _____ One hundred out of 1,000 baby sea turtles grow to become adults.

   _____ The worst dangers that green sea turtles face are from humans.

3. What does the green sea turtle baby use to get out of its shell?

   _____

4. What are some of the natural enemies of the sea turtle?

   _____

5. What information from the passage suggests that if the green sea turtle survives, it lives a long life?

   _____

6. Which of the following pieces of information does this passage not provide?

   A. why sea turtles go back to the beach   **B.** how sea turtles hatch
   C. the dangers sea turtles face in the sea   **D.** how much adult sea turtles weigh

7. How can humans act more responsibly to help the young sea turtles survive?

   _____

   _____

   _____

8. Write three questions you have about the green sea turtle that are not answered in this passage. Consider using the Internet or books to find the answers to your questions.

   _____

   _____

   _____

9. On another sheet of paper, tell how the author feels about the dangers humans add to the life of the young sea turtle. Cite examples from the passage to support your writing. Share your writing with a friend.

ESP: Fact or Fiction?

Even though you haven't talked to your cousin all year, somehow when the phone rings, you know it's her. Later, you are watching a TV show, and before the show gets to its surprise ending, you already know what is going to happen. The next day, you go to the mall with your brother, and while you are still in the parking lot, you suddenly feel that he's going to find a blue shirt and buy it. And, he does!

Do you have **extrasensory perception** (ESP)? ESP is the ability to predict something that will happen or to read another person's mind. ESP involves getting information from a sense other than sight, sound, taste, touch, or smell. It is considered by some as the "sixth" sense.

In the 1930s, a scientist named J. B. Rhine tested subjects to see if they had ESP. He used a set of five cards. Each card had a simple picture: a plus sign, a square, a circle, a star, or three wavy lines. Rhine would look at a card and think hard about the picture on the card. The subject would try to determine which picture Rhine was looking at by reading his mind. Because there were five cards, the subject had a one out of five chance of guessing the right card. If the subject got four out of five cards correct, Rhine thought that showed that the person had ESP. Some people thought that Rhine's test was **unscientific**. They thought the results could be based on **coincidence** or luck.

What do you think? Is ESP science or coincidence?

extrasensory: beyond the senses
perception: observation
unscientific: not having to do with science
coincidence: an unplanned, or accidental, random event

ESP: Fact or Fiction?

Even though you haven't talked to your cousin all year, somehow when the phone rings, you know it's her. Later, you are watching a TV show, and before the show gets to its surprise ending, you already know what is going to happen. The next day, you go to the mall with your brother, and while you are still in the parking lot, you suddenly feel that he's going to find a blue shirt and buy it. And, he does!

Do you have **extrasensory perception** (ESP)? ESP is the ability to predict something will happen or to read another person's mind. ESP involves getting information from a sense other than sight, sound, taste, touch, or smell. It is considered by some as the "sixth" sense.

In the 1930s, a scientist named J. B. Rhine tested subjects to see if they had ESP. He used a set of five cards. Each card had a simple picture: a plus sign, a square, a circle, a star, or three wavy lines. Rhine would look at a card as he thought hard about the picture on the card, trying to "transport" that picture to the subject's mind. The subject would try to determine which picture was on the card by reading Rhine's mind. Because there were five cards, each subject had a one out of five chance of guessing the right card. If the subject got four out of five cards correct, Rhine determined that the person had ESP. Some people thought that Rhine's test was **unscientific** because it was too simplistic, and the results could be based on pure **coincidence** or luck.

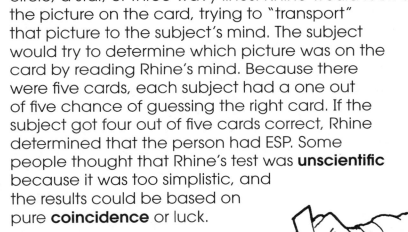

What do you think? Is ESP science or coincidence?

---

extrasensory: beyond the senses
perception: observation
unscientific: not having to do with science
coincidence: an unplanned, or accidental, random event

ESP: Fact or Fiction?

Even though you haven't talked to your cousin all year, somehow when the phone rings, you know it's her. Later, you are watching a TV show, and before the show gets to its surprise ending, you already know what is going to happen. The next day, you go to the mall with your brother, and while you are still in the parking lot, you suddenly get an overwhelming sense that he's going to find a blue shirt and buy it. And, he does!

Do you have extrasensory perception (ESP)? ESP is the ability to predict something will happen before it does or to read another person's mind. ESP involves getting information from a sense other than the usual five senses: sight, sound, taste, touch, or smell. This extrasensory perception is considered by some as the "sixth" sense.

In the 1930s, a scientist named J. B. Rhine tested subjects to see if they had ESP. He used a set of five cards, each with a simple picture: a plus sign, a square, a circle, a star, or three wavy lines. Rhine would look at a card; as he thought hard about the picture on the card, he tried to **telepathically** "transport" that picture to the subject's mind. The subject would try to determine which picture was on the card by reading Rhine's mind. Because there were five cards, the subjects had a one out of five chance of selecting the right card. If the subject got four out of five cards correct, Rhine determined that the subject had ESP. Some people thought that Rhine's test was **unscientific** because it was too simplistic, and the results could be based on pure **coincidence**.

Do you think ESP is science or coincidence?

telepathically: to communicate from one mind to another
unscientific: not having to do with science
coincidence: an unplanned, or accidental, random event

Name _____

6.RI.6, 6.W.1, 6,L,1, 6.L.4

ESP: Fact or Fiction?

Answer the questions.

1. What is ESP? Circle the best definition.

    A. reading cards with symbols on them   **B.** knowing the ending to a TV show
    C. the ability to predict what will happen   **D.** seeing a picture in your mind

2. Read each sentence. Write **F** for fact and **O** for opinion.

    _____ ESP is scientific because it is so interesting.

    _____ Scientists do not believe in ESP.

    _____ J. B. Rhine created a test to try to determine if a person had ESP.

    _____ Some people do not believe in ESP.

3. What does the word *subject* mean as used in this passage? Circle the correct answer.

    A. the servant of a king or leader   **B.** a person whose responses or answers are studied
    C. the main topic of a report   **D.** a field of study in school

4. Why did some people think that J. B. Rhine's test was unscientific? Write your answer in a complete sentence.

    _____

5. Write the root word for each of the following words. Use a dictionary if needed.

    A. unscientific _____   **B.** extrasensory _____

    C. coincidence _____

6. Read the sentence, "J. B. Rhine tested subjects to see if they had ESP." Whom does the pronoun *they* refer to?

    _____

7. Read the sentence, "Do you have extrasensory perception (ESP)?" Why is ESP enclosed in parentheses?

    _____

8. Why is ESP considered a *sixth* sense by some people?

    _____

9. On another sheet of paper, write an expository paragraph beginning with the topic sentence you wrote in question 8. Support your topic sentence with clear reasons and relevant evidence.

© Carson-Dellosa · CD-104618 · Differentiated Reading for Comprehension   19

Mysterious Triangle

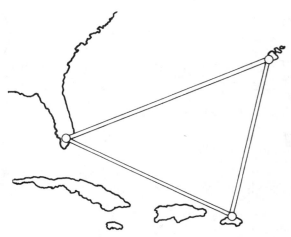

On a map, draw a line from Miami, Florida, to Bermuda. Bermuda is an island in the Atlantic Ocean. Draw a second line from Bermuda to Puerto Rico. Finish by drawing a third line from Puerto Rico to Miami. This makes a triangle over the sea. This triangle is called the Bermuda Triangle.

Stories are told about strange things that happen there. Ships vanish. Planes lose their way. The ship carrying the **treaty** to end the War of 1812 was lost. This delayed the end of the war. In 1945, a group of five airplanes flew over the triangle. These planes were never heard from again. There are many other stories of missing planes and ships.

Why do so many airplanes and ships disappear in this area? There are many different **theories**. Some think that UFOs are to blame. They think the UFOs pick up ships or airplanes. Some say that the lost city of Atlantis is under the sea there. They think the city has a power that pulls ships and planes to it.

Those theories are interesting. But, are there **scientific** theories that could explain why this area is dangerous? Some think that the mystery of the Bermuda Triangle can be explained by the weather. The Bermuda Triangle is a place that has many storms. These storms can form quickly. Wind and rain make steering very hard. Sometimes, boaters and pilots get into trouble because of the sudden storms.

The strangest thing about the Bermuda Triangle is linked to magnets. A compass is supposed to point to magnetic north. But, in the Bermuda Triangle, a compass points to *true* north. No one knows why this happens. This difference can make it easier for ships and planes to get lost and in trouble.

treaty: a formal agreement
theories: guesses or ideas
scientific: agreeing with the principles of science

Mysterious Triangle

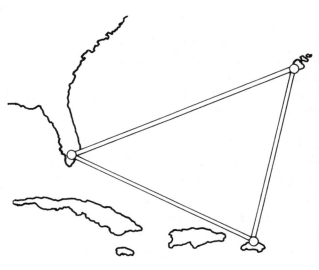

On a map, draw a line from Miami, Florida, to the island of Bermuda in the Atlantic Ocean. Draw a second line from Bermuda to Puerto Rico. Finish by drawing a third line from Puerto Rico to Miami. This makes a triangle over the sea. This triangle is called the Bermuda Triangle.

Stories are told about strange things that happen there. Ships vanish. Planes lose their way. A ship carrying the peace **treaty** from the United States to England to end the War of 1812 was lost, delaying the end of the war. In 1945, a group of five airplanes flew into the triangle and was never heard from again. There are many other stories of missing planes and ships.

Why do so many airplanes and ships disappear in this area? There are many different **theories**. Some people think that UFOs are to blame. They think the UFOs pick up ships or airplanes. Some people say that the lost city of Atlantis is under the sea there. They think the city has a power that pulls ships and planes to it.

Those theories are interesting. But, are there **scientific** theories that could explain why this area is dangerous? Some people think that the mystery of the Bermuda Triangle can be explained by the weather. The Bermuda Triangle is a place that has many storms. These storms can form quickly. Wind and rain make steering very hard. Sometimes, boaters and pilots get into trouble because of the sudden storms.

The strangest thing about the Bermuda Triangle is linked to magnets. A compass is supposed to point to magnetic north. But in the Bermuda Triangle, a compass points to *true* north. No one knows why this happens. This difference can make it easier for ships and planes to get lost and in trouble.

treaty: a formal agreement
theories: guesses or ideas
scientific: agreeing with the principles of science

Mysterious Triangle

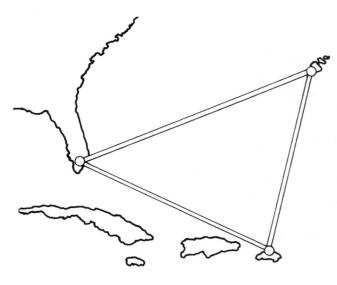

On a map, draw a straight line from Miami, Florida, to the island of Bermuda in the Atlantic Ocean. Draw a second line from Bermuda to Puerto Rico and a third line from Puerto Rico to Miami. These lines form an area called the Bermuda Triangle.

Stories are told about strange occurrences in the Bermuda Triangle. Many ships have vanished, and planes have lost their way in this mysterious triangle. A ship carrying the peace **treaty** from the United States to England to end the War of 1812 was lost, delaying the end of the war. In 1945, a group of five airplanes flew into the triangle and was never heard from again. There are many other stories of missing planes and ships.

Why do so many airplanes and ships disappear in this area? There are many different **theories**. Some think that UFOs fly over the Bermuda Triangle and **intercept** the ships or airplanes. Some people say that the lost city of Atlantis is under the sea there. They think the city has a power that pulls ships and planes to it.

Those theories are interesting; but, are there **scientific** explanations for the disappearance of boats and planes in this area? Some think that the mystery of the Bermuda Triangle can be explained by the weather in the area. The Bermuda Triangle is a place that has many storms. These storms can form instantaneously. Wind and rain make steering difficult, causing trouble for boaters and pilots.

The strangest thing about the Bermuda Triangle is linked to magnets. A compass is supposed to point to magnetic north; but, in the Bermuda Triangle, a compass points to *true* north. No one knows why compasses work differently in this area; the difference can make it easier for ships and planes to get off course.

treaty: a formal agreement
theories: guesses or ideas
intercept: to stop and seize something before it reaches its destination
scientific: agreeing with the principles of science

Mysterious Triangle

Answer the questions.

1. What is the Bermuda Triangle? Write your answer in a complete sentence.

   _____

2. Which of the following events from the passage is *not* a fact?

   A. UFOs pick up ships and planes that pass through the Bermuda Triangle.
   B. A ship carrying a peace treaty to end the War of 1812 disappeared.
   C. Five planes flew over the Bermuda Triangle, never to be seen again.
   D. Compasses in the Bermuda Triangle point to magnetic north instead of true north.

3. The passage presents the following theories for the disappearance of ships and planes in the Bermuda Triangle. Write **S** beside the scientific theories and **U** beside the unscientific theories.

   _____ The weather in the area changes quickly.

   _____ UFOs have been spotted in the area.

   _____ Compasses do not work in the usual way in the Bermuda Triangle.

   _____ Atlantis pulls ships and planes into the ocean.

4. Rewrite the sentence: *Some think that UFOs are to blame.* Replace the pronoun *some* with an antecedent.

   _____

5. Rewrite the sentence: *Some think that the mystery of the Bermuda Triangle can be explained by the weather.* Replace the pronoun *some* with an antecedent.

   _____

6. Write a quotation someone might say about the Bermuda Triangle. Use correct capitalization and punctuation with the quotation marks.

   _____

7. What do you think happened to the ships and planes that disappear in the Bermuda Triangle? Support your opinion with facts.

   _____

   _____

   _____

8. On another sheet of paper, write a story about a ship or plane that enters the Bermuda Triangle. Be sure to engage your readers by creating interesting characters and a well-structured sequence of events.

The Lost City of Z

In 1906, Colonel Percy Fawcett was sent to Bolivia. Bolivia is a country in South America. It is covered with mountains and rain forests. Fawcett's job was to **chart** the unexplored wilderness. Fawcett knew that the job was filled with danger. Travel was hard. There were many diseases. And, the natives were not friendly. But, Fawcett was an adventurer. He looked forward to the challenge of exploring in a land yet uncharted.

Fawcett faced many **hardships**. Hiking through the rain forest was difficult. The **foliage** of the rain forest was thick. Floating a boat down the river was even harder. Fawcett swam across rivers filled with man-eating fish. He was bitten by vampire bats. He risked his life daily.

After three years, his job was finished. But, Colonel Fawcett wanted to keep exploring. He had heard many stories about the Lost City of Z. He had heard that it was older than the pyramids in Egypt. The city was said to be built of stone. There were mines filled with gold. He thought this ancient city might be in the rain forests of Brazil. He spent almost 20 years looking for this lost city.

In 1926, Colonel Fawcett set out once again to find the Lost City of Z. This time, his son joined him. This would be Fawcett's final trip into the rain forest. He and his son were never seen again. No one knows what happened to Fawcett and his son. Search parties tried to find them but were unsuccessful.

Even today, the rain forests of Bolivia and Brazil remain mostly unexplored. The City of Z has never been found.

chart: to make a map
hardships: difficulties
foliage: plants

The Lost City of Z

In 1906, Colonel Percy Fawcett, an Englishman, was sent to Bolivia, a country in South America. It was his job to **chart** the unexplored wilderness of the country. Much of Bolivia is covered with mountains and rain forests. Fawcett knew that the job would be filled with danger. Travel was hard in Bolivia. There were many illnesses. And, the natives there were not friendly. But, Fawcett was an adventurer. He looked forward to the challenge of exploring in a land yet uncharted.

As expected, Fawcett faced many **hardships** as he traveled through the rain forest. It was hard to hike through the forest's **dense foliage**. It was even harder to take a boat over the river rapids. He swam across rivers filled with man-eating fish. He was bitten by vampire bats. He risked his life daily to chart this yet unknown world.

After three years, his job was finished, but Colonel Fawcett wanted to keep exploring. He had heard many stories about the Lost City of Z. He had heard that it was older than the pyramids in Egypt and built entirely of stone. There were rumors that mines near the city were filled with gold. He thought this ancient city might be in the rain forests of nearby Brazil. He spent almost 20 years trying to learn more about the ruins of this city. In 1926, Colonel Fawcett set out with his son on what would be his final trip to find the lost city. The colonel and his son were never heard from again. No one knows exactly what happened to them.

Even today, the rain forests of Bolivia and Brazil remain mostly unexplored, and the City of Z has never been found.

chart: to make a map
hardships: difficulties
dense: thick
foliage: plants

The Lost City of Z

In 1906, Colonel Percy Fawcett, an Englishman, was sent to Bolivia, a country in South America. He was tasked with the job of **charting** the unexplored wilderness of the country. Because much of Bolivia is covered with mountains and rain forests, Fawcett knew that the job would be filled with danger. But, Fawcett was an adventurer. He looked forward to the challenge of exploring in a land yet uncharted.

As expected, Fawcett faced many hardships as he charted the rain forest. The forest's **dense foliage**, the steep ascent up the mountains, and the river rapids made travel difficult through the country. The animals native to the area also posed risks. He encountered man-eating fish and vampire bats. There were many diseases, and the native people did not welcome newcomers on their land. He risked his life daily to chart this yet unknown world.

After three years, his job was finished, but Colonel Fawcett wanted to keep exploring. He had heard many stories about a **legendary** city he called the Lost City of Z. He had heard that it was older than the pyramids in Egypt and built entirely of stone. There were rumors that mines near the city were filled with gold. He thought this ancient city might be in the rain forests of nearby Brazil. He spent almost 20 years trying to learn more about and locate the ruins of this city. In 1926, Colonel Fawcett set out with his son on what would be his final trip into the jungles of South America. He and his son were never heard from again. No one knows exactly what happened to them, but many stories surround their disappearance.

Even today, the rain forests of Bolivia and Brazil remain mostly unexplored, and the Lost City of Z has never been found.

charting: mapping
dense: thick
foliage: plants
legendary: told about in a story from the past or myth

Name _____

The Lost City of Z

Answer the questions.

1. What is the Lost City of Z?

    A. a city in Bolivia   **B.** a city in Brazil

    C. a place that Colonel   **D.** a legendary city said to have gold
       Fawcett mapped

2. The passage states that Colonel Fawcett was an adventurer. Give two examples that support this statement.

_____

_____

3. Why did Colonel Fawcett first go to Bolivia?

    A. to find rubber trees for   **B.** to map the unexplored places
       a British company   in Bolivia

    C. to find the Lost City of Z   **D.** to discover gold

4. Why did Colonel Fawcett stay in Bolivia after his job was finished?

    A. He wanted to learn a new language.

    B. He wanted to go river rafting.

    C. He wanted to find an ancient, lost city.

    D. He wanted to build a new home for his family.

5. Write a complete sentence to tell what people say the Lost City of Z looked like.

_____

6. If the City of Z did exist at one time, what do you think might have happened to it?

_____

7. Circle the best definition for the word *chart* as used in the passage.

    A. a table that shows information   **B.** a map

    C. to make a map   **D.** to plan

8. Fawcett faced many hardships. Describe a hardship you have faced.

_____

_____

9. On another sheet of paper, draw a Venn diagram comparing and contrasting the place where you live to Bolivia.

10. On another sheet of paper, use the information you wrote in your Venn diagram in question 9 to write a paragraph comparing and contrasting the place where you live to Bolivia.

Flying and Spying

Do you like watching spy movies or reading spy books? In books and movies, spying may seem like fun. But in real life, spying is serious business. **Technology** continues to improve spy work. Today, spies may use spy planes. This is one common form of spy technology.

There are many types of spy planes. Each kind does a different type of work. One type of spy plane is used to listen. These planes fly over countries and ships using their radar to gather information. The planes are also equipped with sensors and dish antennas that pick up messages. Some antennas can listen to telephone calls and even pick up faxes. Spies then spend hours analyzing the information to see what is important.

Other planes take pictures, just like satellites do. But, airplanes can fly closer to the ground than satellites can. The pilots must be careful, though. It is against the law to fly over some countries. If the country is unfriendly, the plane might be forced to land.

Spy planes come in many sizes. The government of Israel invented tiny unmanned spy planes that fly without pilots onboard. The smallest of these planes weighs only three pounds (1.36 kg). It can be carried in a backpack and launched **remotely** in any location. Then, the spy uses a laptop computer to **navigate** the plane. The spy can fly the small plane through a window. Inside, the plane takes pictures. The pictures are then sent to the computer. The spy uses the pictures to gather information.

technology: scientific invention
remotely: from a distance
navigate: to steer

Flying and Spying

Do you like watching spy movies or reading spy books? In books and movies, spying may seem like fun, but in real life, spying is serious business. **Technology** continues to improve spy work. Today, a spy plane is one common form of spy technology.

There are many types of spy planes. Each kind does a different type of work. One of the most common spy planes is used to listen in on private conversations and meetings. These planes fly over countries and ships using their radar to gather information. The planes are also equipped with sensors and dish antennas that pick up messages. Some antennas can listen to telephone calls and even pick up faxes. Spies then spend hours analyzing the information to see what is important.

Other planes take pictures, just like satellites do. But, airplanes can fly closer to the ground than satellites can. The pilots must be careful, though. It is against the law to fly over some countries. If the country is unfriendly, the plane might be forced to land.

Spy planes come in many sizes. The government of Israel invented tiny spy planes that fly without pilots onboard. The smallest one weighs only three pounds (1.36 kg). It can be carried in a backpack and launched **remotely** in any location. Then, the spy uses a laptop computer to **navigate** the plane. The spy can maneuver the small plane through a window and take pictures inside a building. The pictures are then sent instantly to the computer to provide the spy with information.

technology: scientific invention
remotely: from a distance
navigate: to steer

Flying and Spying

Do you enjoy watching spy movies or reading spy books? In books and movies, spying may seem like fun, but in real life, spying is serious business. **Technology** continues to improve spy work making it easier to gather important information. Today, a spy plane is a common form of spy technology.

There are many types of spy planes, each designed for a different kind of job. One of the most common spy planes is used to listen in on private conversations and meetings from far away. These planes fly over countries and ships using their radar to gather information. The planes are also equipped with sensors and dish antennas that pick up messages. Some antennas can listen to telephone calls and even pick up faxes. Spies then spend hours analyzing the information to see what is important.

Other planes take pictures, just like satellites do. These planes are able to fly closer to the ground than satellites can. The pilots must be careful, though. It is against the law to fly over some countries. If the country is unfriendly, the plane might be forced to land.

Spy planes come in many sizes. The government of Israel invented tiny unmanned spy planes that fly without pilots onboard. The smallest one weighs only three pounds (1.36 kg) and can be carried in a backpack and launched **remotely** in any location. The specially-trained spy uses a laptop computer to **navigate** the plane. The skilled spy can maneuver the small plane through a window to take pictures inside a building. The pictures are then sent instantly to the computer to provide the spy with information.

technology: scientific invention
remotely: from a distance
navigate: to steer

Flying and Spying

Answer the questions.

1. What does the title, "Flying and Spying," refer to?

   A. satellites used for spying
   C. spy planes as a common spy technology
   B. how to spy on airplane passengers
   D. spies who fly planes

2. The passage states that spying is *serious business*. Cite evidence from the passage and other sources that support this idea.

   _____

   _____

3. Which of the following best describes the most common kind of spy plane?

   A. a plane that gathers information from private conversations and meetings
   B. a plane that flies low and fast over other countries
   C. a plane that sends information to other countries
   D. any plane that a spy flies on

4. What features might a spy plane have?

   _____

5. Write three words or phrases from the passage that describe Israel's spy plane.

   _____

6. What do you think the author of the passage thinks about spy planes? Cite evidence from the passage to support your opinion.

   _____

7. Do you think it is important to have spy planes? Why or why not? Write your answer in complete sentences.

   _____

   _____

8. Who is the audience this passage is written to?

   _____

9. Cite evidence from the passage to support your answer to question 8.

   _____

10. On another sheet of paper, rewrite this passage for a younger audience. Use the style, vocabulary, and organization needed for this audience. Share your writing with someone in your target audience and ask for feedback. Revise if necessary.

Cars of the Future

Today, most cars run on gas. But, many people think that cars of the future will use a different type of fuel. Scientists are trying to develop a way to power cars that would be better for the environment and cheaper than gas. They hope to create a car that runs longer for less money.

People continue to **debate** about what the new fuel should be. Some say electricity is a good fuel. They say it is better for the environment. We already put motors that run on electricity into machines that used to run on gas. We also put electric motors in **hybrid** cars.

Electric cars have a problem. When a car runs out of gas, the driver buys more. But with an electric car, it takes time to charge the battery. Many people do not want to wait for batteries to recharge before they can continue driving.

Fuel cells are another way to fuel cars. Like batteries, fuel cells create energy with a chemical reaction. Unlike batteries, fuel cells don't need to be recharged. These cells run on liquid hydrogen. The liquid hydrogen is then changed into gas. The fuel-cell car cannot go as fast as a gas car. But, it can drive about 120 miles (193.12 km) before it needs more fuel. That is a lot farther than gas-powered cars. Fuel-cell cars also do not pollute the air.

The biggest problem with fuel-cell cars is the cost. Building these cars is expensive. Changing all of the gas stations into fuel-cell stations would be expensive. Right now, if you drove a fuel-cell car, you would have no place to buy hydrogen when it runs out. Figuring out where to get the hydrogen for the cars is also a concern.

What do you think the cars of the future will be like?

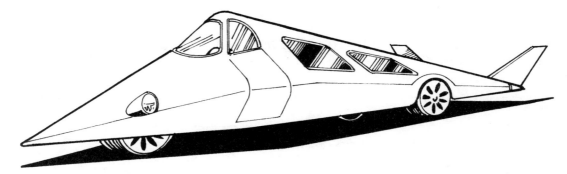

debate: to discuss with differing opinions
hybrid: a vehicle powered by a combustion engine and an electric motor
fuel cell: a machine that changes the chemical energy of fuel

Cars of the Future

Today, most cars run on gas, but many people think that cars of the future will use a different type of fuel. Scientists are trying to develop a way to power cars that would be better for the environment and cheaper than gas.

People continue to **debate** about what the new fuel should be. Some people say electricity would be a good fuel. They say it is better for the environment. We already put motors that run on electricity into machines that used to run on gas, such as lawn mowers. We also put electric motors in **hybrid** cars.

Electric cars have a problem. When a car runs out of gas, the driver buys more, but when an electric car runs down, it takes time to recharge the battery. Many people do not want to wait for batteries to charge before they can continue driving.

Fuel cells are another idea for fueling cars. Like batteries, fuel cells create energy with a chemical reaction. Unlike batteries, fuel cells don't need to be recharged. These cells run on liquid hydrogen, which can be changed into a gas. The fuel-cell car cannot go as fast as a gas car, but it can drive about 120 miles (193.12 km) before it needs more fuel. That is a lot farther than gas-powered cars. Fuel-cell cars also do not pollute the air.

The biggest problem with fuel-cell cars is the cost. Building these cars is expensive. Changing all of the gas stations into fuel-cell stations would be expensive too. Right now, if you drove a fuel-cell car, you would have no place to buy hydrogen when it runs out. Figuring out where to get the hydrogen for the cars is also a concern.

What do you think the cars of the future will be like?

debate: to discuss with differing opinions
hybrid: a vehicle powered by a combustion engine and an electric motor
fuel cell: a machine that changes the chemical energy of fuel

Cars of the Future

Today, most cars run on gas, but many people think that cars of the future will use a different type of fuel. Scientists are trying to develop a fuel and a car that would be better for the environment and cheaper than gas.

People continue to **debate** about what the new fuel should be. Some people say electricity is a good fuel because it is better for the environment. We already put motors that run on electricity stored in batteries into machines that used to run on gas, such as lawn mowers. We also put electric battery-operated motors in **hybrid** cars.

Electric cars sound good in theory, but they do pose a **dilemma** that many drivers cannot overcome. When a car runs out of gas, the driver buys more, but when an electric car runs down, it takes time to recharge the battery. Many people do not want to wait for batteries to charge before they can continue driving.

Fuel cells are another idea for fueling cars without gas. Like batteries, fuel cells create energy with a chemical reaction. Unlike batteries, fuel cells do not need to be recharged. These cells run on liquid hydrogen, which can be changed into a gas. The fuel-cell car cannot go as fast as a gas car, but it can drive about 120 miles (193.12 km) before it needs more fuel. That is a lot farther than gas-powered cars. Fuel-cell cars also do not pollute the air.

The biggest problem with fuel-cell cars is the cost. Building these cars is expensive, not to mention the cost of changing all of the gas stations into fuel-cell stations. Right now, if you drove a fuel-cell car, you would have nowhere to buy hydrogen when it runs out. Figuring out where to get the hydrogen for the cars is also a concern.

What do you think the cars of the future will be like?

debate: to discuss with differing opinions
hybrid: a vehicle powered by a combustion engine and an electric motor
dilemma: problem

Cars of the Future

Answer the questions.

1. Why are scientists looking for other ways to power cars? Write your answer in a complete sentence.

   _____

2. What are the pros and cons of electric cars?

   _____

   _____

3. What are the pros and cons of fuel-cell cars?

   _____

   _____

4. Write **T** for true or **F** for false.

   _____ Hybrid cars run using electric motors.

   _____ Electric cars may be better for the environment than gas-powered cars.

   _____ Liquid hydrogen must be changed into a gas to work in a fuel cell.

   _____ People make liquid hydrogen at home.

5. Which of the following best describes the author's point of view in this passage?

   A. The author is presenting both the pros and cons of each type of fuel.
   B. The author is showing that electric cars are the best for the environment and should be the only cars on the roads.
   C. The author is showing that gas cars are the only practical solution.
   D. The author is showing that fuel-cell cars are a good investment for our future.

6. Choose the definition for the word *charge* as used in this passage.

   A. the cost of something   **B.** to put off paying until a later date
   C. to attack   **D.** to fill with power

7. What type of fuel presented in this passage or from another source do you think would be the best for powering a car?

   _____

8. On another sheet of paper, write an expository essay to support your answer to question 7. Introduce your opinion in the first sentence. Then, support your opinion in an organized manner using the evidence from your research.

A Mind for Math

Are you good at math? Can you multiply numbers in your head? How about 7,686,369,774,870 times 2,465,099,745,799? Shakuntala Devi **calculated** that problem in only 28 seconds. And, she did it without using a paper or pencil.

Shakuntala was a famous math **whiz** from India. She came from a poor family. She had very little schooling. But by three years old, she could solve hard math problems. Her father loved performing card tricks. By learning the order of the cards, Shakuntala would know what card he was going to pull from the deck.

Shakuntala was so good at numbers that she performed her skills in front of audiences. By the time she was eight years old, she had traveled all over India showing her math skills. She performed many kinds of math problems. She could even do calendar problems. If someone said a date in history, Shakuntala could figure out the day of the week that date fell on.

Shakuntala was born in 1939. When she was young, computers were really big. One computer would fill a whole room. Shakuntala could **compute** math problems faster than those big computers. She was able to find the square root of a 201-digit number faster than a computer.

Shakuntala thought that most people used computers and calculators too much. She believed that the brain needs exercise. Shakuntala thought the use of computers or calculators slowed the brain. She encouraged students to not use calculators until college. That way, their brains could get a good workout.

calculate: to figure out using mathematics

whiz: a person who is good at a particular activity

compute: to figure out, often by using a computer or calculator

A Mind for Math

Are you good at math? Can you multiply numbers in your head? How about 7,686,369,774,870 times 2,465,099,745,799? Shakuntala Devi **calculated** that problem in only 28 seconds without using a paper or pencil. She was a mathematical **phenomenon**.

This famous mathematician from India came from a poor family. She had very little schooling. But by three years old, she could solve hard math problems. Her father loved performing card tricks. By learning the order of the cards and remembering them, Shakuntala would know what card he was going to pull from the deck.

Shakuntala was so good at numbers that she performed her skills in front of audiences. By the time she was eight years old, she had traveled all over India showing her math skills. She performed many kinds of math problems. She could even do calendar problems. If someone said a date in history, Shakuntala could figure out the day of the week that date fell on.

Shakuntala was born in 1939. When she was young, computers were really big. One computer would fill a whole room. Shakuntala could **compute** math problems faster than those early computers. She was able to find the square root of a 201-digit number 10 seconds faster than a computer.

Shakuntala thought that most people used computers and calculators too much. She believed that the brain needs exercise just like other parts of the body. Shakuntala thought the use of computers or calculators slowed the brain. She encouraged students to not use calculators until college. That way, their brains could get a good workout.

calculate: to figure out using mathematics
phenomenon: someone or something that is very impressive
compute: to figure out, often by using a computer or calculator

A Mind for Math

Are you good at math? Can you multiply numbers in your head? How about 7,686,369,774,870 times 2,465,099,745,799? That's just one problem that Shakuntala Devi **calculated** in her head in only 28 seconds without using a pencil and paper. She was a mathematical **phenomenon**.

This famous mathematician from India came from a poor family. She had very little schooling, but by the time she was three years old, she could solve hard math problems. Her father loved performing card tricks. By learning the order of the cards and remembering them, Shakuntala would know what card he was going to pull from the deck.

Shakuntala was so good at numbers that she performed her skills in front of audiences. By the time she was eight years old, she had traveled all over India showing her mathematical skills. She could do all kinds of math problems including calendar problems. If someone said a date in history, Shakuntala could instantly figure out the day of the week that date fell on.

Shakuntala was born in 1939. When she was young, computers were so large and **cumbersome** that one computer would fill a whole room. Shakuntala could **compute** math problems faster than those early computers. She was able to find the square root of a 201-digit number 10 seconds faster than a computer.

Shakuntala thought that most people used computers and calculators too much. She believed that the brain needs exercise just like other parts of the body. Shakuntala thought students should not use computers or calculators until they went to college. That way, their brains could get a good workout.

calculated: to figure out using mathematics
phenomenon: someone or something that is very impressive
cumbersome: bulky
compute: to figure out, often by using a computer or calculator

A Mind for Math

Answer the questions.

1. This passage tells about Shakuntala Devi's gift for mathematics. Write three sentences from the passage that support this main idea.

   _____

   _____

   _____

2. Write **T** for true or **F** for false.

   _____ Shakuntala needed to use a calculator for big numbers.

   _____ Shakuntala could do math faster than early computers.

   _____ Shakuntala Devi was from India.

   _____ Shakuntala came from a rich family.

   _____ Shakuntala memorized the order of cards in her father's card tricks.

3. Write two synonyms from the passage for the word *calculate*.

   _____

4. Write another synonym for the word *calculate*, not found in this passage. Use a dictionary or thesaurus.

   _____

5. Write the word from the passage that describes a person with a remarkable gift.

   _____

6. Write a sentence telling about something you are good at. Use the vocabulary word you wrote in question 5.

   _____

7. Write a 21-digit number on the line below. Then, ask a classmate to try to read it aloud.

   _____

8. Why did Shakuntala think students should not have computers or calculators until they are in college? Write your answer in a complete sentence.

   _____

9. Do you agree with Shakuntala's belief stated in question 8? On another sheet of paper, write your response. Be sure to begin by stating your opinion in a sentence. Then, follow your opinion with reasons and evidence.

A Life in Poetry

Mattie Stepanek was born with a **burden** and a gift. The burden was a disease called muscular dystrophy (MD), a serious condition that makes the muscles weak. It also makes it hard to breathe. Children with this disease have a short **life expectancy**. But, besides this disease, Mattie had a gift—his love for life.

Instead of feeling sorry for himself, Mattie lived his life fully. He wrote poetry and gave speeches. He first created poems when he was only three years old. He spoke his poems into a tape recorder because he was too little to write them down. Later, when he was able to write, he wrote essays and stories too. He called his **inspirational** book of poems *Heartsongs*. The books of his poems became best sellers.

Mattie also worked to help other children who had MD. He spoke at events for MD and helped raise money for research. Because he had a rare kind of MD, the doctors learned a lot from studying him. Through research, doctors and scientists hope to one day find a cure for this disease. From his wheelchair, he worked hard to help other people. "People tell me I inspire them," Mattie said once. "And, that inspires me. It's a beautiful circle."

Mattie died in June 2004, at the age of 13, but his books and his life continue to inspire people. Mattie's brave view of life helped him to make a difference. Mattie said that a hero never gives up. If that is true, then Mattie Stepanek was a hero who had an amazing life.

burden: difficulty
life expectancy: the number of years a person is expected to live
inspirational: able to affect feelings or thought

A Life in Poetry

Mattie Stepanek was born with a **tremendous burden** and a beautiful gift. The burden was a disease called muscular dystrophy (MD), a serious condition that makes the muscles weak. It also makes it difficult to breathe. Children with this disease have a short **life expectancy**. But, besides this disease, Mattie had a gift—his positive attitude and his love for life.

Instead of feeling sorry for himself, Mattie lived his life fully. He wrote poetry and gave speeches. He first created poems when he was only three years old. He spoke his poems into a tape recorder because he was too little to write them down. Later, when he was able to write, he wrote essays and stories, too. He collected his **inspirational** poems into best-selling books called *Heartsongs*.

From his wheelchair, Mattie worked hard for the cause by speaking at events for MD and helping to raise money for research. Because he had a rare kind of MD, the doctors learned a lot from studying him. Through research, doctors and scientists hope to one day find a cure for this disease. "People tell me I inspire them," Mattie said once. "And, that inspires me. It's a beautiful circle."

Mattie died in June 2004, at the age of 13, but his books and his life continue to inspire people. Mattie's brave view of life helped him to make a difference. Mattie said that a hero never gives up. If that is true, then Mattie Stepanek was a hero who had an amazing life.

tremendous: great or large
burden: difficulty
life expectancy: the number of years a person is expected to live
inspirational: able to affect feelings or thought

A Life in Poetry

Mattie Stepanek was born with both a tremendous **burden** and a beautiful gift. The burden was the disease of muscular dystrophy (MD)—a serious condition that weakens the muscles and makes it difficult to breathe without the aid of an oxygen tube. Children with this disease have a short **life expectancy**. But, besides this disease, Mattie had a gift—his positive attitude and his love for life.

Instead of feeling sorry for himself, Mattie lived his life fully. He demonstrated his positive attitude through his poetry and speeches. He began creating poems when he was only three years old. At first, he spoke his poems into a tape recorder because he was too little to write them down. Later, when he was able to write, he wrote essays, stories, and speeches too. He collected his **inspirational** writings into best-selling books called *Heartsongs*.

From his wheelchair, Mattie continued to work hard for the cause of muscular dystrophy by speaking at MD events and helping to raise money for research. He met and inspired others with the disease as well as many famous people. "People tell me I inspire them, and that inspires me. It's a beautiful circle," Mattie said. Because he had a rare kind of MD, the doctors learned a lot from studying him. Through research, doctors and scientists hope to one day find a cure for this disease.

Mattie died in June 2004, at the age of 13, but he lived his 13 years more fully than some who live many more years. His books and his life continue to inspire people around the world. Mattie's brave view of life helped him to make a difference in the lives of the people who knew him. Mattie once said that a hero never gives up. If that is true, then Mattie Stepanek lived the life of a **valiant** hero.

---

burden: difficulty
life expectancy: the number of years a person is expected to live
inspirational: able to affect feelings or thought
valiant: brave

Name _____

6.RI.2, 6.RI.6, 6.W.3, 6.W.5, 6.L.5

A Life in Poetry

Answer the questions.

1. The author of this passage contrasted Mattie's burden with his gift.

    A. What was Mattie's burden? _____

    B. What was his gift? _____

2. What is *muscular dystrophy*?

    A. a disease that weakens the muscles
    B. a disease that weakens the brain
    C. a disease that affects a person's blood
    D. a condition that causes people to love life

3. Write three words or phrases from the passage that describe Mattie.

    _____

4. What was one way that Mattie helped other people? Write your answer in a complete sentence.

    _____

5. Do you think the author of the passage knew Mattie or knew about Mattie? Provide reasons to support your answer.

    _____

    _____

6. Did Mattie's story inspire you? Explain your answer.

    _____

    _____

7. Write the name of someone you know who has inspired you.

    _____

8. Write three qualities you admire about the person you named in question 7.

    _____

9. On another sheet of paper, write a narrative about the person you named in question 7. Develop each quality you wrote in question 8 in its own paragraph using descriptive words, quotations, and experiences.

10. Read your narrative to a friend. Ask for suggestions on how to improve your writing. Revise your writing using your friend's suggestions. Ask your friend to sign on the line below.

© Carson-Dellosa · CD-104618 · Differentiated Reading for Comprehension   43

The Sun at the Center

Because of his careful scientific work, Galileo Galilei is called the Father of Science. But, it is his understanding of our solar system that he is most known for. He was the first person to take a long, close look at our night sky.

In 1592, most people believed that Earth was in the center of the universe. They believed that the sun, the stars, and the planets **revolved** around Earth. Galileo questioned this idea. He had heard of another scientist named Copernicus who thought that the sun was in the center of our solar system. But, Copernicus could not prove this idea. Galileo was very good at thinking about and solving problems. He would turn each problem into a few, simple questions. Then, he would look for the answers. That is what he did with Copernicus's idea.

Galileo knew he needed a telescope to begin his work. The telescope had been invented a few years before, but telescopes were not easily available. So, Galileo made one of his own. His telescope was even better than the original one. He used his telescope to observe the changes in the night sky. He wrote about his **observations**. Galileo wrote about seeing mountains on the moon. He was the first to see that the Milky Way was not a cloud of gas but actually a group of hundreds of thousands of stars. He also saw shadows on Venus that changed like the phases of the moon. From this, Galileo **concluded** that Venus must travel around the sun and not around Earth.

Galileo's study of the night sky helped to prove that the sun is at the center of the solar system. He proved that the Earth, along with the other planets and moons, revolves around the sun.

revolve: move in a curving orbit around a center
observations: notes of things that have been seen
concluded: determined based on facts

The Sun at the Center

Because of his careful scientific work, Galileo Galilei is called the Father of Science. But, it is his understanding of our solar system that he is most known for. He was the first person to take a long, close look at our night sky.

In 1592, most people believed that Earth was in the center of the universe. They believed that the sun, the stars, and the planets **revolved** around Earth. Galileo questioned this **theory**. He had heard of another scientist named Copernicus who thought that the sun was in the center of our solar system. But, Copernicus could not prove his theory. Galileo was very good at thinking about and solving problems. He would turn each problem into a few, simple questions. Then, he would look for the answers and **proof**. That is what he did with Copernicus's idea.

Galileo knew he needed a telescope to begin his work. The telescope had been invented a few years before, but telescopes were not easily available. So, Galileo made one of his own. His telescope was even better than the original one. He used his telescope to observe the changes in the night sky. He **documented** his observations. Galileo wrote about seeing mountains on the moon. He was the first to see that the Milky Way was not a cloud of gas but actually a group of hundreds of thousands of individual stars. He also saw shadows on Venus that changed like the phases of the moon. From this, Galileo concluded that Venus must travel around the sun and not around Earth.

Galileo's study of the night sky helped to prove that the sun is at the center of the solar system and that Earth, along with the other planets and moons, revolves around the sun.

> **revolve:** move in a curving orbit around a center
> **theory:** a scientific idea not yet proven to be true or false
> **proof:** evidence that something is true
> **documented:** wrote about

The Sun at the Center

Because of his careful scientific work, Galileo Galilei is called the Father of Science, but it is his understanding of our solar system that he is most known for. He was the first person to take a long, close look at our night sky.

In 1592, most people believed that Earth was in the center of the universe and that the sun, the other stars, and the planets **revolved** around Earth. Galileo questioned this **theory**. He had heard of another scientist named Copernicus who thought that the sun was in the center of our solar system, but Copernicus could not prove his theory. Galileo was very good at thinking about and solving problems. He would turn each problem into a few, simple questions or terms and then look for the answers and **proof**. That is what he did with Copernicus's idea.

Galileo knew he needed a telescope to begin his work. Since the telescope had just been invented a few years before, they were not easily available, so Galileo made one of his own. His telescope was even better than the original one. He used his telescope to observe the planets and **documented** his observations. Galileo wrote about seeing mountains on the moon and the details of the Milky Way. He was the first to see that the Milky Way was not a cloud of gas but actually a group of hundreds of thousands of individual stars. He also saw shadows on Venus that changed just like the phases of the moon. From this, Galileo concluded that Venus must travel around the sun and not around Earth.

Galileo's study of the night sky helped to prove that the sun is at the center of the solar system and that Earth, along with the other planets and moons, revolves around the sun.

revolve: move in a curving orbit around a center
theory: a scientific idea
proof: evidence that something Is true
documented: wrote about

The Sun at the Center

Answer the questions.

1. What was the author's purpose in writing this passage?

    A. to persuade the reader to study science
    B. to inform the reader about the work of Galileo
    C. to inspire the reader to become an astronomer
    D. to entertain the reader with a funny story

2. The passage states that Galileo is known for *his careful scientific work*. Write two details from this passage that support this statement.

   _____

   _____

3. Which of the following best describes Copernicus's theory of our solar system?

    A. He believed that the sun rose and set in the sky.
    B. He believed that the sun, not Earth, was the center of our solar system.
    C. He believed that the planets stayed in one place as the sun moved around them.
    D. He believed that the stars guided the planets through the solar system.

4. Write three things that Galileo observed with his telescope.

   _____

   _____

   _____

5. Locate information about Galileo on the Internet or in a book or magazine. Write the source on the line below.

   _____

6. Write two ideas from your additional source that support the information in the passage.

   _____

   _____

7. Write one new idea from your additional source that is not included in the passage.

   _____

8. On another sheet of paper or on the computer, write a report on Galileo using information from the passage and your additional source. Include the quote you wrote in question 9. Cite your sources including the passage in this book on a separate page of your report.

A Love of the Ocean

Even as a child, Robert Ballard loved the ocean. Growing up on the coast of California, he loved looking at ocean life. He enjoyed wading in **tidal** pools. He later went to college to learn more about the ocean.

After college, Robert continued to follow the call of the ocean. He served in the US Navy. He then moved to the coast of Massachusetts, where he worked as an **oceanographer**. He was given a special project to explore the ocean floor. He mapped its underwater mountain ranges. He also invented a special **submarine** to help him map the ocean floor. He loved exploring the deep ocean. It was exciting work. He and his team found plants that were able to live without sunlight. They found fish that no one knew existed. But, Robert had another project in mind.

Robert wanted to find the *Titanic*—the great ship that sank on its first **voyage**—and had dreamed of finding it for years. For more than 70 years, people had looked unsuccessfully for the sunken ship. Robert thought he could find the *Titanic*. In 1985, Robert and his crew spent a whole summer looking for the missing ship. His ship went back and forth across the water where he thought that the great ship might be. After a few months, his search equipment showed pictures of a huge shape on the floor of the ocean. He had found the *Titanic*.

Unfortunately, the weather was getting bad, and the sea was too rough to safely explore the *Titanic* up close. Robert had to wait a whole year until he could go back. Then, he got into a tiny submarine and dove slowly into the dark water. It took more than two hours to reach the *Titanic*. Robert was the first person to see the ship since the day it sank.

tidal: having to do with tides, the regular rising and falling of water
oceanographer: a person who studies the ocean
submarine: an underwater ship
voyage: trip

A Love of the Ocean

Even as a child, Robert Ballard loved the ocean. Growing up on the coast of California, he loved looking at ocean life and wading in **tidal** pools. He later went to college to learn more about the sea and the life underneath the waves.

After college, Robert continued to follow the call of the ocean. He served in the US Navy. He then moved to the coast of Massachusetts, where he worked as an **oceanographer**. He was given a special project to explore the ocean floor. He mapped its underwater mountain ranges. He also invented a special **submarine** to help him map the ocean floor. He loved exploring the deep ocean life. It was exciting work. He and his team found plants that were able to live without sunlight and fish that no one knew existed. But, Robert had another project in mind.

Robert wanted to find the *Titanic*—the great ship that sank on its first **voyage**—and had dreamed of finding it for years. For more than 70 years, people had searched unsuccessfully for the sunken ship. Because of his mapping work and his special submarines, Robert thought that he could find the *Titanic*. In 1985, Robert and his crew spent a whole summer looking for the missing ship. His ship went back and forth across the water where he thought that the great ocean liner might be. After a few months, his search equipment sent back pictures of a huge shape on the floor of the ocean. He had found the *Titanic*.

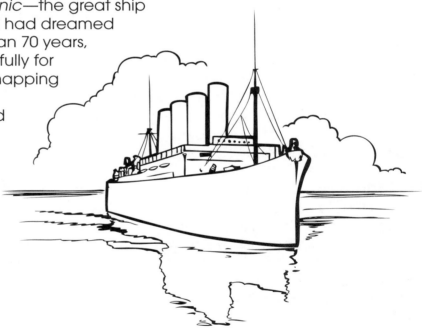

tidal: having to do with tides, the regular rising and falling of water
oceanographer: a person who studies the ocean
submarine: an underwater ship
voyage: trip

A Love of the Ocean

Even as a child, Robert Ballard loved the ocean. Growing up on the coast of California, he loved looking at ocean life and wading in **tidal** pools of the Pacific Ocean. He later went to college to learn more about the sea and the life underneath the waves.

After college, Robert continued to follow the call of the ocean. He served in the US Navy. He then moved to Massachusetts along the coast of the Atlantic Ocean, where he worked as an **oceanographer**. He was given a special project to explore the ocean floor and map the underwater mountain ranges. He invented a special **submarine** to help him make a map of the ocean floor. He and his team found plants that were able to live without sunlight and fish that no one knew existed. They made many interesting discoveries. It was exciting work. Although he loved exploring the deep ocean life, Robert had another project in mind.

Robert wanted to find the *Titanic*—the huge ocean liner that sank in 1912 on its first **voyage** across the Atlantic Ocean—and had dreamed of finding it for years. For more than 70 years, people had searched unsuccessfully for the sunken ship. But because of his mapping work and his special submarines, Robert thought that he could find the *Titanic*. In 1985, Robert and his crew spent a whole summer going back and forth across the water looking for the missing ship. Then, on September 1, 1985, his search equipment sent back pictures of a huge shape on the floor of the ocean. He had found the *Titanic*.

tidal: having to do with tides, the regular rising and falling of water
oceanographer: a person who studies the ocean
submarine: an underwater ship
voyage: trip

Name _____

A Love of the Ocean

Answer the questions.

1. The title of this passage is "A Love of the Ocean." Give three examples of Robert Ballard's love of the ocean.

_____

_____

_____

2. Write **T** for true and **F** for false.

_____ Robert Ballard is an inventor and a scientist.

_____ Much of Robert's life was spent near or on the ocean.

_____ Robert found mapping the ocean floor boring.

_____ Before Robert Ballard's search, people knew exactly where the *Titanic* was.

3. Write the pronoun used to describe each antecedent below.

   A. Robert _____   **B.** Robert and his team _____   **C.** work _____

4. Write the sentence from the passage that uses dashes to set off a parenthetical phrase.

   _____

5. The Greek root *graph* means *to write*. Write the vocabulary word that contains the root *graph*. Explain how this root provides a clue to the word's meaning.

   _____

6. The prefix *sub* means *under* or *below*. Write the vocabulary word that contains the prefix *sub*. Explain how its prefix provides a clue to the word's meaning.

   _____

7. Write a question you have after reading this passage.

   _____

8. Research the answer to the question you wrote in question 7. Write the answer and the source on the lines below.

   _____

   _____

9. Use the information from this passage and the research you did to answer the question you wrote in question 7 to write a research report at least three pages in length. Publish your report using the computer.

Gateway to the Oceans

In the 1800s, ships had to make the long trip around the tip of South America to get from the Atlantic Ocean to the Pacific Ocean. The ships often faced huge, dangerous storms. People knew that building a **canal** would make these trips shorter and safer. A canal through Central America could save 8,000 miles (12,875 km) on a trip from New York to San Francisco. In Panama, a country in southern Central America, only 50 miles (80 km) of land separates the two oceans. This was an ideal place for a canal.

Some work started on the canal in 1880. But, the work could not be completed. It was not until 1914 that a successful **gateway** connected the two seas. Work on the canal was not easy. It took thousands of workers. It took millions of dollars. Because of the mountains, the canal had to be built with locks. Locks are **chambers** that fill with water or drain it away. Locks move a ship up and down through the canal. When a ship enters the canal, big, thick gates close at each end of the chamber. Water pours through pipes and the locks raise the ship as much as 85 feet (25.91 m). Then, the gates facing the front of the ship open. The ship moves safely to the next chamber. The Panama Canal has 12 chambers.

Today, more than 40 ships go through the Panama Canal each day. The ships wait in line for their turn. It can take up to 10 hours for a ship to travel through the canal. Most of the ships carry products such as grain, iron ore, and new cars. Some ships carry passengers. More than one-quarter of a million passengers travel through the Panama Canal each year.

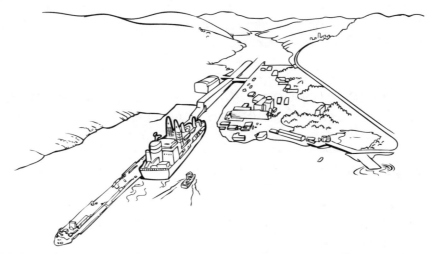

canal: narrow waterway that connects two large bodies of water
gateway: an entrance or passage
chamber: a small space or section inside a canal

Gateway to the Oceans

In the 1800s, ships had to make the long trip around the tip of South America to get from the Atlantic Ocean to the Pacific Ocean. The ships often faced huge, dangerous storms. People knew that building a **canal** would make these trips shorter and safer. A canal through Central America could save 8,000 miles (12,875 km) on a trip from New York to San Francisco. In Panama, a country in southern Central America, only 50 miles (80 km) of land separate the two oceans.

Some work started on the canal in 1880, but it could not be completed. It was not until 1914 that a successful **gateway** connected the two seas. Work on the canal was not easy. It took thousands of workers and millions of dollars to dig the Panama Canal. Because of the mountains, the canal had to be built with locks. Locks are **chambers** that fill with water or drain it away. Locks move a ship up and down through the canal. When a ship enters the canal, big, thick gates close at each end of the chamber. Water pours through pipes and the locks raise the ship as much as 85 feet (25.91 m). Then, the gates facing the front of the ship open. The ship moves safely to the next chamber. Panama Canal has 12 chambers.

Today, more than 40 ships go through the canal every day. It can take up to 10 hours for a ship to travel from one end of the canal to the other. The ships wait in line for their turn. Most of the ships carry cargo such as grain, iron ore, new cars, and other products. Some ships also carry passengers. More than one-quarter of a million passengers travel through the great canal every year.

canal: narrow waterway that connects two large bodies of water
gateway: an entrance or passage
chamber: a small space or section inside a canal

Gateway to the Oceans

In the 1800s, ships had to make the long, **arduous** voyage around the tip of South America to get from the Atlantic Ocean to the Pacific Ocean. The ships often faced many hardships including huge, dangerous storms. People knew that building a canal through Central America would make these voyages shorter and safer. A **canal** through Central America could save 8,000 miles (12,875 km) on a trip from New York to San Francisco. In Panama, a small country in southern Central America, only 50 miles (80 km) of land separated the two oceans. This was the ideal place for a canal.

Some work started on the canal in 1880, but it could not be completed. It was not until 1914 that a successful **gateway** finally connected the two seas. Work on the canal was not easy. It took thousands of workers and millions of dollars to dig the Panama Canal. Because of the mountains between the two oceans, the canal had to be built with locks, or **chambers**, that fill with water or drain it away. Locks move a ship up and down through the canal. When a ship enters the canal, big, thick gates close at each end of the chamber. Water pours through pipes and the locks raise the ship as much as 85 feet (25.91 m). Then, the gates facing the front of the ship open. The ship moves safely to the next chamber. The Panama Canal has 12 chambers.

Today, more than 40 ships go through the Panama Canal every day. It can take up to 10 hours for a ship to travel from one end of the canal to the other. The ships wait in line for their turn. Most of the ships carry cargo such as grain, iron ore, new cars, and other products. Some ships carry passengers. More than one-quarter of a million passengers travel through the great canal every year.

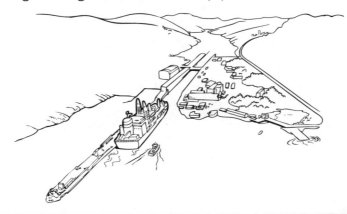

arduous: difficult, full of hardships
canal: narrow waterway that connects two large bodies of water
gateway: an entrance or passage
chamber: a small space or section inside a canal

Name _____

6.RI.2, 6.W.3, 6.L.3, 6.L.5

Gateway to the Oceans

Answer the questions.

1. What is the author's purpose for writing this passage?

   A. to persuade the reader to travel by ship
   B. to inspire the reader to build more canals to make ocean travel easier
   C. to entertain the reader with an exciting story about a voyage on a ship
   D. to inform the reader about the building of the Panama Canal

2. Why was the Panama Canal built? Write your answer in a complete sentence.

   _____

   _____

3. Why was Panama the ideal place to dig the canal?

   _____

4. Read the following statement: *Work on the canal was not easy.* Circle all of the answers that support the statement.

   A. It took thousands of workers to build the canal.
   B. The mountains in Panama made the building of the canal even harder.
   C. More than a quarter million passengers travel through the canal each year.
   D. It cost millions of dollars to build the canal.

5. Why was the Panama Canal built with locks?

   A. The locks are needed for faster travel.
   B. The locks raise and lower ships at each point along the canal.
   C. The locks help heavy ships pass through the canal.
   D. The locks are not necessary.

6. Write **T** for true and **F** for false.

   _____ The Panama Canal was finished in 1904.

   _____ The canal cut 8,000 miles (12,875 km) off a trip from New York City to San Francisco.

   _____ The Panama Canal contains 12 lock chambers.

   _____ It can take 10 days to get through the Panama Canal.

7. How does the author's use of numbers add interest to the passage?

   _____

8. On another sheet of paper or on the computer, write a story about the Panama Canal. After completing your story, count the words in each sentence. If the lengths of your sentences do not vary, revise your writing to provide interest for the reader.

Enormous Statues

When Dutch explorers first spied Easter Island, they thought that the island was haunted. It looked so **ominous**. Unlike most tree-covered islands in the Pacific Ocean, this small island had bare hills. Surrounding the hills were giant statues that looked like men with huge heads and little bodies. There are more than 880 statues on the island. Each statue had its own platform and stood between 10 and 40 feet (3.05 and 12.19 m) tall. Some stand in rows with their backs to the sea. Others are pushed over and broken. The mystery of the **massive** statues and the strange, bare island took hundreds of years to solve.

Today, some **archaeologists** think that Easter Island was made **barren** because of the statues. They believe that when people first came to the island between AD 400 and AD 700, it was green and covered with forests. Clues left on the island show that the native people made big boats from the trees. They caught large fish to eat. They made ropes from a tree called *hauhau*. They planted crops. But then, they started to make statues.

No one is sure why the statues were made. It might have been to honor dead ancestors. But, it is believed that the native people carved more and more statues. They cut down trees and used the logs to roll the statues into place. Clans competed with each other to make the best statues. By about 1400, most of the trees on the island were gone. Without trees, animals could not live there any longer. The natives could no longer build boats and get food from the sea. The good soil washed away, so they could not grow crops. Most of the people and animals disappeared from Easter Island, leaving behind only the enormous statues.

ominous: threatening
massive: very large
archaeologist: a scientist who studies ancient people and cultures
barren: empty; without plants

Enormous Statues

When Dutch explorers first spied Easter Island, they thought that the island was haunted. It looked so **ominous**. Unlike most tree-covered islands in the Pacific Ocean, this small island had bare hills. Surrounding the hills were more than 880 **massive** statues that looked like men with huge heads and little bodies. Each giant statue, called *moai*, has its own platform called *ahu* and stands between 10 and 40 feet (3.05 and 12.19 m) tall. Some statues stand in rows with their backs to the sea, and others lay broken. The mystery of the huge statues and the strange, bare island took hundreds of years to solve.

Today, some **archaeologists** think that Easter Island was made **barren** because of the statues. They believe that when people first came to the island between AD 400 and AD 700, it was green and covered with forests. Clues left on the island show that the native people made big boats from the trees and caught large fish to eat. They made ropes from a tree called *hauhau*. They planted crops. But then, they started to make statues.

No one is sure why the statues were made. It might have been to honor dead ancestors. But, it is believed that the native people continued to carve more and more statues. They cut down trees and used the logs to roll the statues into place. Clans may have competed with each other to make the best statues. By about 1400, most of the trees on the island were gone. Without trees, the animals died, the natives could no longer build boats and get food from the sea, and the good soil washed away. Without good soil, the people could not grow crops. Over time, most of the people and animals disappeared from Easter Island, leaving behind only the enormous statues.

ominous: threatening
massive: very large
archaeologist: a scientist who studies ancient people and cultures
barren: empty; without plants

Enormous Statues

When Dutch explorers first spied Easter Island off the coast of South America, they thought that the island was haunted. Unlike most tree-covered islands in the Pacific Ocean, this small island with bare hills looked **ominous**. Surrounding the hills were more than 880 **massive** statues that looked like men with huge heads and little bodies. Each giant statue, called *moai*, has its own platform called *ahu* and stands between 10 and 40 feet (3.05 and 12.19 m) tall. Some statues stand in rows with their backs to the sea, and others lay broken on the ground. The mystery of the massive statues and the strange, bare island took hundreds of years to solve.

Today, some **archaeologists** think that Easter Island was made **barren** because of the statues. They believe that when people first came to the island between AD 400 and AD 700, the island was green and covered with forests. Clues left on the island show that the native people made big boats from the trees, caught fish, and planted crops. They made ropes from a tree called *hauhau*. But then, they started to make the enormous statues.

No one is sure why the statues were made. It might have been for religious reasons or to honor dead ancestors. Clans may have competed with each other to make the biggest and best statues. But, it is believed that once the native people started making statues, they continued to carve more and more of them. They cut down the trees and used the logs to roll the statues into place. By about 1400, most of the trees on the island were gone. Without trees, the animals could not live, the natives could no longer build boats and get food from the sea, and the good soil washed away. Without good soil, the people could not grow crops. Over time, most of the people and animals disappeared from Easter Island, leaving behind only a few of the native people and the enormous statues.

ominous: threatening
massive: very large
archaeologist: a scientist who studies ancient people and cultures
barren: empty; without plants

Enormous Statues

Answer the questions.

1. What is the author's purpose for writing this passage?

   A. to persuade the reader to not cut down trees
   B. to inspire the reader to visit Easter Island
   C. to inform the reader about how the large statues originated on Easter Island
   D. to entertain the reader with an exciting story about a haunted island

2. Why did the Dutch explorers think that Easter Island was haunted?

   _____

3. What evidence provided in the passage supports archaeologists' belief that Easter Island was once green and covered with trees?

   _____

4. Circle the best summary for this passage.

   A. Easter Island is known for its huge stone statues.
   B. Easter Island's huge stone statues may have ruined life on the island.
   C. Archaeologists make up stories to explain what life was like long ago.
   D. Today, Easter Island has no trees.

5. This passage describes the enormous statues found on Easter Island. Write three synonyms for the word *enormous* used in the passage. Then, look in a thesaurus to find one more synonym.

   _____

6. Write a word from this passage that is an antonym for the words *tree-covered*.

   _____

7. Write descriptive phrases from the passage to compare how Easter Island looked before and after the statues.

   _____
   _____
   _____

8. Use the Internet, books or magazines to find reasons that experts think may been why the natives of Easter Island built the large statues. On another sheet of paper or on the computer, write an informational passage about the statues on Easter Island. Include the reason you think the natives built the statues.

Time Stood Still

The town of Pompeii was once a busy port on the Bay of Naples on the coast of Italy. It was a part of the great Roman Empire. On the morning of August 24, AD 79, the people of Pompeii woke for the last time in their beautiful town.

Mount Vesuvius stood behind the town. The people of Pompeii did not know the mountain was actually a volcano until it blew. First, a cloud of smoke and ash shot into the air. It blocked the sun. It burned the trees. Next, volcanic rocks rained on the town. Some people ran away. Others thought that it was safer to stay inside their houses. They thought that the rocks and ash would eventually stop falling.

The rocks and ash did stop falling, but not until the town was almost buried. Then, something much worse happened. Fiery volcanic mud and red-hot **magma** shot out of the volcano and **surged** toward the town. When the blast hit Pompeii, the people who stayed in their homes were buried. Finally, the magma cooled into hard rock, creating a hard, closed **tomb** over the city.

Thousands of people were killed that day. The people who escaped returned weeks later to find that the whole town was buried. They tried to dig tunnels into the town to find their houses and the bodies of those who had died, but it was too hard.

Pompeii remained undisturbed until the 1700s when archaeologists started to dig up the buried town. The ash and mud had protected the city. Whole houses were still standing. The paintings on the walls were still clear. Scientists could even make casts of the bodies that they found. The casts were so detailed that they showed the expressions on the people's faces. Time stood still that day in Pompeii.

magma: hot liquid rock from a volcano
surge: flow forward suddenly, like a wave
tomb: a place where the dead are buried

Time Stood Still

The town of Pompeii was once a bustling port on the Bay of Naples on the coast of Italy. It was a part of the great Roman Empire. On the morning of August 24, AD 79, the people of Pompeii woke for the last time in their beautiful town.

Mount Vesuvius stood behind the town. The people of Pompeii did not know the mountain was actually a volcano until it blew. First, a cloud of smoke and ash shot into the air. It blocked the sun and burned the trees. Next, volcanic rocks rained on the town. Some people ran away while others thought that it was safer to stay inside their houses. They thought that the rocks and ash would eventually stop falling.

The rocks and ash did stop falling, but not until the town was buried. Then, something much worse happened. Fiery volcanic mud and red-hot **magma** shot out of the volcano and **surged** toward the town. When the blast hit Pompeii, the people who stayed in their homes were buried. Finally, the magma cooled into hard rock, creating a hard, closed **tomb** over the city.

Thousands of people were killed that day. The people who escaped returned weeks later to find that the whole town was buried under the hard volcanic rock. They tried to dig tunnels into the town to find their houses and the bodies of those who had died, but it was impossible.

Pompeii remained undisturbed until the 1700s when archaeologists started to dig up the buried town. The ash and mud had protected the city, leaving whole houses still standing. Paintings on the walls were still clear. Scientists could make casts of the bodies that they uncovered. The casts were so detailed that they even showed the expressions on the people's faces. Time stood still that day in Pompeii.

magma: hot liquid rock from a volcano

surge: flow forward suddenly, like a wave

tomb: a place where the dead are buried

Time Stood Still

Pompeii was a bustling port on the Bay of Naples on the coast of Italy and an important city in the great Roman Empire until the morning of August 24, AD 79. That's when the people of Pompeii woke for the last time in their beautiful town.

Adding to the beauty of Pompeii, Mount Vesuvius stood behind the coastal town. The people of Pompeii did not know the mountain was actually a volcano until that **fateful** day. First, and without warning, a cloud of smoke and ash shot high into the air. It blocked the sun and burned the trees. Next, volcanic rocks rained on the town. Some people ran away while others thought that it was safer to stay inside their houses; they thought the rocks and ash would eventually stop falling.

The rocks and ash did stop falling, but not until the town was almost buried. Then, something even more horrific happened. Fiery volcanic mud and red-hot **magma** shot out of the volcano and **surged** toward the town. When the blast hit Pompeii, the people who stayed in their homes were buried. Finally, the magma cooled into hard rock, creating a hard, closed **tomb** over the city.

Thousands of people were killed that day. The people who escaped returned weeks later to find that the whole town was buried under the hard volcanic rock. They tried to dig tunnels into the town to find their houses and the bodies of those who had died, but it was impossible.

Pompeii remained undisturbed until the 1700s when archaeologists started to dig up the buried town. The ash and mud had protected the city, leaving whole houses still standing. Paintings on the walls were still clear. Scientists could make casts of the bodies that they uncovered. The casts were so detailed that they even showed the expressions on the people's faces. Time stood still that day in Pompeii.

fateful: happening without one's control, usually with a bad result
magma: hot liquid rock from a volcano
surge: flow forward suddenly, like a wave
tomb: a place where the dead are buried

● ● ● **Differentiated Reading for Comprehension**

Time Stood Still

Answer the questions.

1. Is "Time Stood Still" a good title for this passage? Explain why or why not.

   _____

2. Write **T** for true and **F** for false.

   _____ Pompeii was destroyed by a flood.

   _____ Pompeii was a town in Greece.

   _____ Pompeii was built on the Bay of Naples.

   _____ Everyone in Pompeii knew that Mount Vesuvius was a volcano.

3. Number the following events from 1 to 5 in the order that they happened in the passage.

   _____ Rocks rained down on the town.

   _____ A cloud of smoke and ash shot into the air.

   _____ The magma cooled into hard rock and covered the town.

   _____ Fiery volcanic mud and magma shot out of the volcano.

   _____ The cloud of smoke and ash blocked the sun and burned the trees.

4. Write the metaphor used to describe the town covered by cooled magma.

   _____

5. What information from the passage can you use to infer the reasons why the townspeople could not dig through the hardened magma to find their homes?

   _____

   _____

6. What did the archaeologists who dug up the town find?

   _____

7. Why was Pompeii so well preserved?

   _____

8. Write four transition words used in this passage.

   _____

9. Read about another volcano explosion on the Internet or in a book or magazine. Take notes. On another sheet of paper or on the computer, compare and contrast the eruption of Mount Vesuvius to the other volcanic explosion you read about. Use transition words to clarify the relationship between ideas.

Answer Key

Page 7

1. strange, unusual, amazing; 2. Answers will vary but may include it was strange looking, flew and dove into the water, and made strange sounds. 3. lives mostly at sea, good diver; 4. like a mooing cow; 5. They use their wings to dive deep into the sea. 6. A puffin lives on land when it is hatching and raising its chicks. 7. F, O, F, O; 8. Answers will vary. 9. Answers will vary but may include clown-like beaks, black feathers, and wings. 10. Answers will vary.

Page 11

1. ferocious, menacing, feared, tough; 2. B; 3. a lion at mealtime; 4. furry; small; sharp teeth; long claws; black, gray, and white skunk-striped fur; 5. Many believe the honeyguide leads the honey badger to the hive and then eats what the honey badger leaves behind. 6. Its long claws help it dig up small animals or eggs underground and climb trees for fruit. Its sharp teeth help it rip open melons. Its scent gland stuns the bees. 7. Answers will vary. 8. Answers will vary. 9. Answers will vary.

Page 15

1. C; 2. F, T, F, T; 3. an egg tooth, or small horn, on its beak; 4. crabs, coyotes, dogs, fish; 5. It can grow to be 500 pounds (226.8 kg). 6. A; 7. Answers will vary but should include leashing their pets, not littering, and pulling in fishing nets. 8. Answers will vary. 9. Answers will vary.

Page 19

1. C; 2. O, O, F, F; 3. B; 4. Some people thought that the results could be based on coincidence or luck. 5. A. science, B. sense, C. incident; 6. subjects; 7. to show the meaning of the acronym that will replace the term; 8. because it gathers information without using sight, sound, touch, taste, or smell; 9. Answers will vary.

Page 23

1. The Bermuda Triangle is an area of the Pacific Ocean between Miami, Puerto Rico, and Bermuda where many boats and ships have disappeared without explanation. 2. A; 3. S, U, S, U; 4. Answers will vary, but a possible answer includes: People think that UFOs are to blame. 5. Answers will vary, but a possible answer includes: Scientists think that the mystery of the Bermuda Triangle can be explained by the weather. 6. Answers will vary. 7. Answers will vary. 8. Answers will vary.

Page 27

1. D; 2. Answers will vary but should include challenges Fawcett faced in the rain forest. 3. B; 4. C; 5. The Lost City of Z was said to be older than the pyramids in Egypt, built of stone, and have mines filled with gold. 6. Answers will vary. 7. C; 8. Answers will vary. 9. Answers will vary. 10. Answers will vary.

Page 31

1. C; 2. Answers will vary but should include cited evidence. 3. A; 4. radar, sensors to pick up messages, dish antennas, cameras; 5. small, weighs three pounds (1.36 kg), can be launched remotely, unmanned, can fly through windows, takes pictures inside buildings; 6. Answers will vary. 7. Answers will vary. 8. sixth-grade students; 9. Answers will vary but may include the vocabulary used, style of writing, and that it is in a sixth-grade reading book. 10. Answers will vary.

Page 35

1. Scientists are looking for other ways to power cars that would cost less and be better for the environment. 2. Pros: good for the environment, technology already available; Cons: time it takes to recharge the battery; 3. Pros: don't need to be recharged, go farther without needing more fuel, do not pollute; Cons:

cost and availability; 4. T, T, T, F; 5. A; 6. D; 7. Answers will vary but should be presented as a thoughtful opinion with reasons. 8. Answers will vary but should be presented as a thoughtful opinion supported with reasons.

Page 39

1. Answers will vary but should include facts from the passage. 2. F, T, T, F, T; 3. multiply, solve, figure, compute; 4. determine, work out, add, subtract, divide; 5. whiz or phenomenon; 6. Answers will vary. 7. Answers will vary. 8. She thought the brain needed to be exercised. 9. Answers will vary.

Page 43

1. A. muscular dystrophy, B. his love of life; 2. A; 3. Answers will vary but could include positive, hard working, a good writer, and inspirational. 4. He spoke at events for MD, helped raise money for research, and inspired others. 5. The author probably just knew about Mattie because there is no reference to knowing him or personal stories. 6. Answers will vary. 7. Answers will vary. 8. Answers will vary. 9. Answers will vary. 10. Answers will vary.

Page 47

1. B; 2. Answers will vary but could include that he looked for proof, he improved the telescope, and he documented his observations. 3. B; 4. changes in the night sky, mountains on the moon, stars in the Milky Way, shadows on Venus; 5. Answers will vary. 6. Answers will vary. 7. Answers will vary. 8. Answers will vary.

Page 51

1. Answers will vary but could include that he loved looking at the ocean and wading in it, he studied the ocean in college, and he joined the US Navy. 2. T, T, F, F; 3. A. he, B. they, C. it; 4. Robert wanted to find the *Titanic*—the great ship that sank on its first voyage—and had dreamed of finding it for years. Or, Robert wanted to find the *Titanic*—the huge ocean liner that sank in 1912 on its first voyage across the Atlantic Ocean—and had dreamed of finding it for years. 5. oceanographer, one who writes about the ocean; 6. submarine, an underwater ship; 7. Answers will vary. 8. Answers will vary. 9. Answers will vary.

Page 55

1. D; 2. The Panama Canal was built to shorten the long, dangerous trip between the Pacific Ocean and the Atlantic Ocean. 3. There is only 50 miles (80 km) of land separating the two oceans. 4. A, B, D; 5. B; 6. F, T, T, F; 7. Answers will vary. 8. Answers will vary.

Page 59

1. C; 2. The hills were bare, and they were lined with huge statues. 3. Clues showed that people made boats from trees and that they made rope from trees. 4. B; 5. huge, giant, massive; Additional synonyms will vary. 6. barren; 7. green and covered with forests before the statues; bare, barren, ominous, haunted after the statues; 8. Answers will vary.

Page 63

1. Answers will vary. 2. F, F, T, F; 3. 3, 1, 5, 4, 2; 4. a hard, closed tomb; 5. Answers will vary but may include that good digging equipment was not invented yet. 6. houses, paintings, bodies; 7. The ash and the mud had protected the city. 8. first, next, then, finally; 9. Answers will vary.